GREAT CITIES
OF THE WORLD

LONDON

GILL STACEY

WORLD ALMANAC® LIBRARY

Please visit our web site at: www.worldalmanaclibrary.com
For a free color catalog describing World Almanac® Library's list of high-quality books
and multimedia programs, call 1-800-848-2928 (USA) or 1-800-387-3178 (Canada).
World Almanac® Library's fax: (414) 332-3567.

Library of Congress Cataloging-in-Publication Data

Stacey, Gill.
    London / by Gill Stacey.
        p. cm. — (Great cities of the world)
    Includes bibliographical references and index.
    Contents: History of London — People of London — Living in London — London at work —
London at play — Looking forward.
    ISBN 0-8368-5022-X (lib. bdg.)
    ISBN 0-8368-5182-X (softcover)
    1. London (England)—Juvenile literature. [1. London (England).] I. Title. II. Series.
DA678.S77 2003
942.1—dc21   2003049693

First published in 2004 by
World Almanac® Library
330 West Olive Street, Suite 100
Milwaukee, WI 53212 USA

Copyright © 2004 by World Almanac® Library.

Produced by Discovery Books
Editor: Gianna Williams
Series designers: Laurie Shock, Keith Williams
Designer and page production: Keith Williams
Photo researcher: Rachel Tisdale
Maps and diagrams: Keith Williams
World Almanac® Library editorial direction: Jenette Donovan Guntly
World Almanac® Library art direction: Tammy Gruenewald
World Almanac® Library production: Beth Meinholz

Photo credits: AKG London: pp.10, 12, 13; AKG London/Richard Booth: p.42; Art Directors and Trip/A. Bartel: pp.4, 30;
Art Directors and Trip/A. Tovy: p.21; Art Directors and Trip/B. Turner: cover, title page; Art Directors and Trip/I. Genut:
p.23; Art Directors and Trip/Ken Powell: p.40; Art Directors and Trip/R.Winstanley: p.18; Chris Fairclough Photography:
pp.27, 29, 33; Corbis: pp.14, 16, 17, 38, 39; Corbis/Carlos Dominguez: p.37; David Simson, DASPhotoGB@aol.com: p.24;
Discovery Picture Library: pp.7 (bottom), 8, 26; Hutchison Library: p.20; Hutchison Library/Robert Francis: p.7 (top);
Hutchison Library/Jeremy Horner: pp.25, 43; Hutchison Library/Tony Souter: p.11; Hutchison Library/Philip Wolmuth:
pp.22, 28; Museum of London: p.9; Panos Pictures: p.32; Still Pictures/Adrian Arbib: p.19; Still Pictures/Dylan Garcia: p.34;
Still Pictures/Mark Edwards: p.35; Still Pictures/Theresa De Salis: p.41

Cover caption: The Queen's Foot Guard on parade in front of Buckingham Palace, London.

Printed in the United States of America

1 2 3 4 5 6 7 8 9 07 06 05 04 03

Contents

Introduction

> "...when a man is tired of London, he is tired of life: for there is in London all that life can afford."
>
> —Dr. Samuel Johnson

London is the capital city both of England and of the United Kingdom of Great Britain (comprising England, Scotland, and Wales) and Northern Ireland. It lies in southeastern England on the Thames River. London is one of the largest cities in Europe, with a population of more than seven million.

◄ *An aerial view of London following the path of the Thames River.*

Tradition and Change

For nearly a thousand years, British monarchs have made London their royal capital. William the Conqueror held his coronation in Westminster Abbey in 1066, and all but two monarchs have been crowned there since. London has several royal palaces, including Buckingham Palace, where the queen lives and works.

London is also the seat of the United Kingdom's government. Members of Parliament meet to debate and pass new laws in the House of Commons in the Palace of Westminster (more commonly called the Houses of Parliament). The most famous address in London is 10 Downing Street, the official residence of British prime ministers since 1732.

London is a dynamic, modern city. Its skyline and architecture are changing, with striking new buildings such as the headquarters of Lloyd's Bank and the London Assembly building. Crumbling Victorian warehouses, once part of London's docks, have been restored as fashionable apartments and offices. The new millennium landmarks—the London Eye and the Millennium Bridge—have become familiar sights along the banks of the Thames River.

Cultural Diversity

London is one of the most ethnically diverse cities in Europe. More than three hundred different languages are spoken

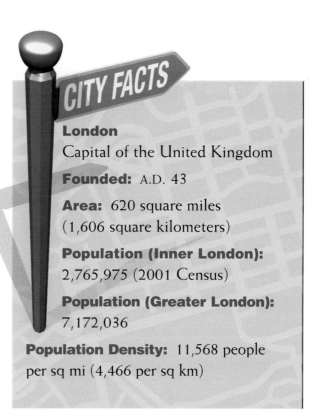

CITY FACTS

London
Capital of the United Kingdom

Founded: A.D. 43

Area: 620 square miles (1,606 square kilometers)

Population (Inner London): 2,765,975 (2001 Census)

Population (Greater London): 7,172,036

Population Density: 11,568 people per sq mi (4,466 per sq km)

there. The influence of this rich mix of peoples can be seen everywhere, in the city's restaurants, markets, festivals, and places of worship.

London is also a city of culture. The choice of entertainment is endless, ranging from world-class theater, West End movie theaters, and classical music to street entertainers, comedy, and dance clubs. The city has many major museums and art galleries.

Like many cities, London often seems overcrowded and noisy, yet more than half the city is green space or water. The royal parks, many public and private gardens, the Thames River, and Regent's Park Canal all offer city dwellers a moment of tranquillity in the middle of a fast-paced city.

Principal Areas of Central London

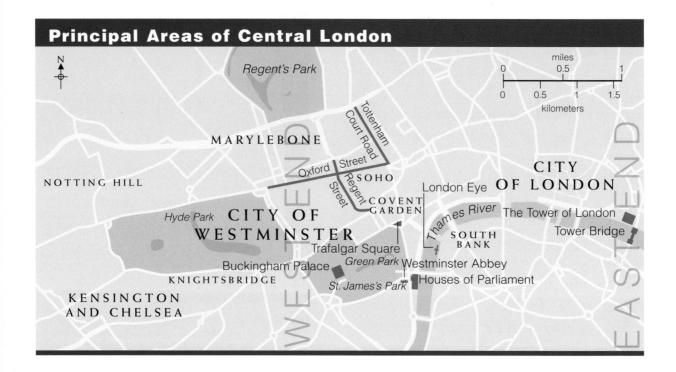

London is a huge and sprawling city. Its size can make it a little overwhelming, both for visitors and for the people who live there. The city has no single central area. Londoners tend to identify with the area they live or work in. People also often think of themselves as North Londoners or South Londoners, depending on whether they live north or south of the Thames River, which divides the city in half. London also has "villages," clearly defined areas with their own small centers, such as Hampstead, Chelsea, Wimbledon, and Clerkenwell.

The "City"

Since 1965, the different districts that make up the whole of London have been officially called "Greater London." Greater London is divided into thirty-two boroughs and the Corporation of the City of London, which often is called just "the City," or the "Square Mile" (because of its size). The City, founded on the original Roman settlement, is the oldest part of London and is rich in history and tradition. It has its own local government and is also the financial and business heart of modern London.

Boroughs

Around the City on both sides of the Thames River are twelve inner London boroughs collectively known as "Inner London." They include the City of Westminster, where many of London's most famous landmarks can be seen: Trafalgar Square and Nelson's Column,

The Thames River

The Thames lies at the heart of London. Over the centuries, London grew into an important, wealthy world city because of its river trade. Twenty-seven bridges cross the Thames in London, including Westminster Bridge, London Bridge, and Tower Bridge. The most recently built bridge, the Millennium Bridge, is for pedestrians only.

The river, once highly polluted, now is so clean over one hundred species of fish live in it.

The Thames is a tidal river, and in places the water can rise 20 feet (6 meters) at high tide. In the past, London was subject to serious flooding from the river. Today, the Thames Barrier (left) at Woolwich protects London from floods. Completed in 1984, it is the largest movable flood barrier in the world.

Buckingham Palace, the Houses of Parliament, and Westminster Abbey. The West End, London's main shopping and entertainment district, is also in the borough of Westminster.

Spreading out around the inner boroughs are twenty outer London boroughs. These are home to two out of every three people who live in the capital.

▼ *Tourists and Londoners enjoy a sunny day in Trafalgar Square. The large building in the background is the National Gallery, a museum of fine art.*

CHAPTER 1

History of London

The first people to live in the London area were probably Celtic tribes native to the British Isles. In A.D. 43, the Romans arrived in Britain from the European mainland and established a fort and trading town, which they called Londinium.

Londinium

In A.D. 60 or 61, Boudicca, queen of the Iceni—a native tribe in eastern England—attacked Londinium. The town was burned to the ground and the inhabitants were massacred. Finally crushed by Roman troops, Boudicca took poison rather than be captured. A statue of Boudicca stands on the Thames embankment, near the Houses of Parliament.

The Romans rebuilt Londinium with strong stone walls to protect it. Over the next three hundred years, Londinium grew into an important port and trading center for the Roman Empire. The city boasted an amphitheater, temples, public baths, paved streets, and luxurious villas.

Decline and Regeneration

As their empire declined in the fifth century, the Romans left Londinium. For several hundred years, the great Roman city was almost deserted, its walls and buildings fell

◀ *The Tower of London. The White Tower (left) was the first part of the tower to be built, on the orders of William the Conqueror, to defend London against invaders and rebellious townspeople.*

▶ *An artist's reconstruction of Roman Londinium in about A.D. 250. The Thames River was much wider then than it is today.*

into ruin, and it suffered attacks from raiding tribes from Scandinavia.

The Anglo-Saxon king who became known as Alfred the Great captured London from the Danes in 886. Under his rule, London became the largest city in Alfred's kingdom of Wessex, which covered the southwest of England. By the beginning of the eleventh century, London had grown to such an extent that King Edward the Confessor built a great abbey and palace at Westminster. This was to become the seat of English monarchs.

The Guilds of the City of London

In the fourteenth and fifteenth centuries, skilled craftsmen formed guilds organized according to trade or crafts. There were nearly a hundred guilds for goldsmiths, tailors, shoemakers, bakers, fishmongers, and others. The guilds became very powerful within the City. They elected the local government and controlled craft standards, wages, and working conditions. Today, 103 guilds meet in the original Guildhall, which was built in the fifteenth century. Parts of it were destroyed during the Great Fire of London (1666) and the bombings of the "Blitz" (1940–1941), but the stone walls survived. The City of London's elected assemblies still meet in the repaired Guildhall, which is also used for state and civic banquets.

Medieval London

In 1066 the Normans, Vikings who had settled in northern France, invaded England. They captured London and William the Conqueror, their leader, was crowned at Westminster. He built fortresses to defend London, including the White Tower, which was part of the Tower of London.

For the next three hundred years, London prospered. The City grew as the heart of London trade and business, while Westminster became the center of government.

Yet London was an unhealthy city. Its streets were crowded and filthy and there was no clean water or sanitation. From 1348 to 1349, a raging epidemic, the Black Death, killed about thirty thousand people, more than half of London's population.

Tudor and Stuart London

The Tudor period began with King Henry VII in 1485. Under the Tudors, London became one of the most powerful and wealthy cities in the world. London's population grew from about 33,000 people in 1500 to about 250,000 people in 1600.

During the Reformation in the sixteenth century, King Henry VIII refused to recognize the authority of the Pope and declared himself Head of the Church of England. Henry abolished Catholic monasteries and gave much of their land to his supporters. This brought great changes to London. Tudor nobles sold off monastery land and became instantly wealthy. A building boom followed. People, new houses, shops, workshops, and industries crowded into the City.

From 1533–1603, the reign of Henry VIII's daughter, Elizabeth I, London saw the Thames River crowded with ships bringing new trade goods from the Americas and Asia. Powerful overseas trading companies were set up, such as the Muscovy Company and the East India Company, bringing great wealth to the British.

Elizabethan London was an exciting city. Theaters, taverns, bearbaiting, and cockfights flourished. William Shakespeare and Christopher Marlowe wrote plays that were performed in London at such famous playhouses as the Rose and the Globe.

The Stuart period began in 1603 when James VI of Scotland became James I of England, and united the two countries.

Stuart London saw many political and religious troubles. Many English Catholics felt they were unfairly treated by the Protestant government. In the 1605 Gunpowder Plot, a group of Catholic rebels tried, unsuccessfully, to blow up the Houses of Parliament.

▼ *A print of London during Elizabeth I's reign shows Old London Bridge crowded with shops and houses.*

The Great Plague and Great Fire

The plague, a fatal disease spread by rat flea bites, was a regular visitor to London's unhealthy streets. In 1665, a vicious outbreak, known as the Great Plague, killed nearly eighty thousand Londoners.

The following year, the Great Fire of London started in a baker's shop on Pudding Lane. Fanned by strong winds, the fire raced through London's tightly packed wooden houses and narrow alleys. The fire burned for four days, destroying four-fifths of the entire city and leaving about one hundred thousand people homeless.

The medieval and Tudor city was gone forever. New buildings of stone and brick replaced those of wood and thatch. Christopher Wren designed most of the new churches, including St. Paul's Cathedral.

Heart of an Empire

By 1700, London's population had risen to roughly five hundred thousand. It was the seat of the British Parliament and the heart of an empire growing in power and wealth.

"One entire arch of fire... of above a mile long...
The churches, houses, and all on fire and flaming
at once, and a horrid noise the flames made,
and the cracking of houses at their ruin..."

—Samuel Pepys, diarist,
on the Great Fire of London.

▲ *St. Paul's Cathedral, designed by Christopher Wren and completed in 1710, took over thirty years to complete. On Wren's tomb inside the cathedral is a Latin inscription that translates: "Reader, if you seek his memorial, look about you."*

London was also the capital of the nation that led the Industrial Revolution at the end of the eighteenth century. As factories were built and businesses grew, more and more people left the countryside to seek work in cities such as London.

As London expanded into new areas, the West End, near Parliament and the royal court, became very fashionable. Elegant new town houses and fine squares, such as Grosvenor Square, were built. The East End grew up around the docks, as trade along the river became increasingly important.

▼ A poor area of London, 1874. People crowded into East End areas such as Whitechapel and Wapping in search of work in the warehouses and docks.

Coffee Houses

During the eighteenth century, London's coffee houses became the place to meet. Here artists, writers, political thinkers, and businessmen gathered to exchange ideas, to gossip, and to conduct business. The London Stock Exchange, at the heart of the City's financial system, was formed in a coffee house. So too were the postal system and many of Britain's first newspapers.

Victorian London

During Queen Victoria's reign, 1837–1901, Britain led the world in industry and trade. The British Empire stretched around the globe. London was the leading world city,

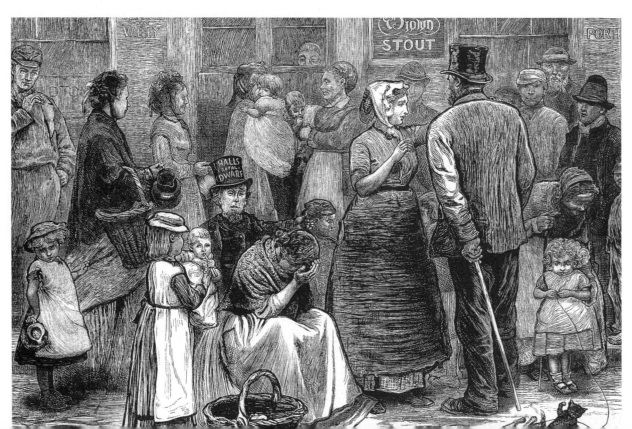

▲ *The London Underground in 1862. The first line was the Metropolitan, which ran from Paddington to the City.*

and its population exploded from about 1 million in 1800 to 6.6 million by 1900. The new railroad networks and the world's first subway system, called the "Underground," allowed families to live in the new suburbs and commute to work. "Greater London" came into existence, although it was not called that until 1965.

As London became more crowded, living conditions worsened. Air pollution from factories and coal fires led to the infamous London smog. Raw sewage and garbage went straight into London's waterways.

"That great foul city of London—rattling, growling, smoking, stinking—ghastly heap of fermenting brickwork, pouring out poison at every pore..."

—John Ruskin, writer and art critic, on 1860s London.

There were frequent epidemics of diseases such as cholera, typhus, and smallpox. The average life expectancy for poorer Londoners was twenty-two. After the 1860s, London became a much healthier place to live, thanks to the engineer Sir Joseph Bazalgette, who designed London's sewage system, still in use today.

Newcomers settled in the poorer areas of London, including more than one hundred thousand Irish, many fleeing the disastrous Great Potato Famine of 1845–1848. Jewish families, escaping persecution in Eastern Europe, found their way to the East End.

Twentieth-Century London

At the beginning of the twentieth century, Britain ruled the largest empire in the world. Londoners enjoyed the gaiety of the theater and the music hall (vaudeville). New elegant restaurants, hotels, and department stores opened, including the Ritz and Selfridge's. With the outbreak of World War I in 1914, thousands of Londoners died on battlefields in Europe.

In the years after World War I, the economy declined and many Londoners lost their jobs.

Yet London continued to grow. New forms of transportation were introduced, including the bus and the car. The Underground was electrified, and new lines were opened, allowing expansion in these areas. At the rural fringes of London, new

"The vast mass of London itself, fought street by street, could easily devour an entire hostile army; and we would rather see London laid in ruins and ashes than that it should be tamely and abjectly enslaved."

—Winston Churchill,
prime minister, July 14, 1940.

housing "estates" (areas of identical small houses with gardens) were built, the suburbs expanded, and cheap "semidetached" houses (houses attached to other houses in pairs) became popular.

World War II

During World War II (1939–1945) the Germans targeted London and its people. The city was bombed relentlessly. Many London children became evacuees, sent away from their London homes to the safety of the countryside. During the "Blitz"—short for "Blitzkrieg," German words meaning "lightning war"—of 1940–1941, German bombers dropped

▼ *London during the "Blitz" of 1940–1941. Smoke rises above Tower Bridge and the Thames River.*

close to 10,000 bombs in nightly raids on London. About 30,000 Londoners died in bombings during the war, and large areas of the city were destroyed.

Postwar London

By 1945, Britain had given up most of its powerful empire. The costs of war had left industries and the docks in decline. The damaged city was rebuilt, but with poorly planned and constructed housing; many inner city areas became run down.

Postwar immigration changed London's population. Workers from the British Commonwealth—the Caribbean, India, Pakistan, Hong Kong, and Cyprus—were encouraged to come to Britain to work, especially in the new National Health Service (a free health-care system set up by the British government in 1948) and for London Transport, which was responsible for running all of London's transportation systems, including the city's bus services and underground trains.

The last decades of the century saw new industries and businesses. In the 1960s, "Swinging London" set world trends in music, art, and fashion, as British celebrities from the Beatles and the Rolling Stones to fashion designer Mary Quant and model Twiggy became internationally famous. London's skyline changed as new high-rise office buildings were built. Areas such as the run-down Docklands were redeveloped, becoming stylish places to live and work.

Living with Terrorism

The Irish Republican Army—or IRA—based in Northern Ireland began attacking targets in London in 1972. Its aim was to force the separation of Northern Ireland from the United Kingdom, uniting it with the Irish Republic.

Bomb threats became common in central London's public places throughout the 1980s and 1990s. In 1992, an IRA bomb destroyed or damaged several office buildings in the City, killing two people and causing $570 million in damage. A year later, a truck bomb killed one person and cost millions more in damage. A "ring of steel" was set up: a network of security checkpoints at which the police monitored every vehicle entering the City. In 1996, the IRA bombed Canary Wharf, one of London's newest building complexes, killing three people.

Between September 2000 and August 2001, another organization, calling itself the "Real IRA," carried out four separate terrorist attacks in London.

Following September 11, 2001, when Islamic terrorists destroyed the World Trade Center in New York City, London was put on alert in case of attacks from similar groups. Military personnel and tanks were sent to guard London's main airport, Heathrow, beginning in 2003.

Royal London

London has many historic buildings, traditions, and ceremonies that are linked

to the British royal family and that are still part of the fabric of London life, even as the political importance of the monarchy has waned.

Palaces

Britain's present queen is Elizabeth II and Buckingham Palace is her official home in London. It has more than six hundred rooms, including the queen's apartment and offices. The State Rooms, where the queen entertains, are now open to the public in the summer. Every year, several thousand people from all walks of life are invited to attend the queen's garden parties in the palace grounds.

Other London buildings with special royal associations include Clarence House, once home of Queen Elizabeth's mother,

▲ *Buckingham Palace was built three hundred years ago as a town house for the Duke of Buckingham. Queen Victoria made it the main royal residence.*

who was known as the Queen Mother, and Kensington Palace, where Princess Diana lived for several years. On the outskirts of London is Hampton Court, a splendid Tudor palace.

The Tower of London

Every day, the Tower of London's famous guards, called Beefeaters, welcome visitors from all over the world to this 1,000-year-old fortress. It has been a royal residence, as well as a prison and a place of execution. Today, it houses the priceless Crown Jewels, used by the royal family on state occasions.

The Queen's Regiments

The queen is colonel-in-chief of seven regiments of the military, known as the Household Regiments. They are her personal troops. The Queen's Foot Guard is responsible for guarding Buckingham Palace. The guards wear bright red uniforms and tall bearskin hats. The daily Changing of the Guard is carried out with great ceremony and military precision.

An even more colorful ceremony is Trooping the Colour, a royal tradition that dates back over two hundred years. Every June, on her official birthday, the queen

▼ *The Queen's Foot Guard performs the Changing of the Guard ceremony at Buckingham Palace every day.*

takes the salute from the Household Regiments. Each year, a different regiment troops its flag (the "Colour") for the queen to inspect.

The Lord Mayor's Show

The Lord Mayor of the City of London is elected annually by members of the ancient guilds. This is one of London's most ancient traditions, dating back to 1215. Every November, the new Lord Mayor travels in a scarlet and gold coach from the City to the Royal Courts of Justice to swear an oath of loyalty to the queen. He is accompanied by floats, guards, and marching bands, in one of the most colorful of London's annual events.

CHAPTER 2

People of London

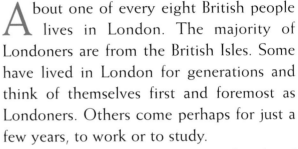

About one of every eight British people lives in London. The majority of Londoners are from the British Isles. Some have lived in London for generations and think of themselves first and foremost as Londoners. Others come perhaps for just a few years, to work or to study.

London is one of the most multicultural cities in the world. The different communities and cultures contribute to the wealth and diversity of London life.

Cockneys

Cockneys are Londoners from the East End. East-Enders can claim to be true Cockneys only if they were born within the sound of Bow Bells, the bells of St. Mary-le-Bow Church in the City. After World War II, many East

Pearly Kings and Queens

Cockneys have their own "royal family," the Pearly Kings and Queens (left), named after the pearl suits they wear. The first Pearly King was Henry Croft, a nineteenth-century road sweeper and rat catcher, who decided to set up a charity to help London's poor. He decorated his clothes with thousands of pearl buttons, in the style of the "costermonger" market sellers he knew, who decorated their clothes with pearls to attract customers. The title of Pearly King or Queen is inherited. They wear their pearl suits for charity events and for their annual festival at St. Martin-in-the-Fields Church in Trafalgar Square.

End families moved to Essex, a county to the east of London, where towns were being built to encourage poor families to leave the city slums. For this reason, there are fewer Londoners today who are true Cockneys.

London's Irish Community

More than one in ten Londoners is of Irish descent. Irish people arrived in London in large numbers in the nineteenth century, fleeing the terrible potato famine of 1845–1848. They worked primarily as laborers, building the roads, railroads, and canals. More came after World War II and played a key role in rebuilding the war-torn capital. Irish Londoners live in all parts of London, with strong communities in areas such as Kilburn in northwest London.

Londoners from Continental Europe

Many people from the different member countries of the European Union and other parts of Europe live and work in London. Most stay no more than a few years. Others have made their homes in the capital, including those in an established Cypriot community. There are also small but distinct communities of Italians and Poles, as well as Jews who came mostly from Germany and Eastern Europe.

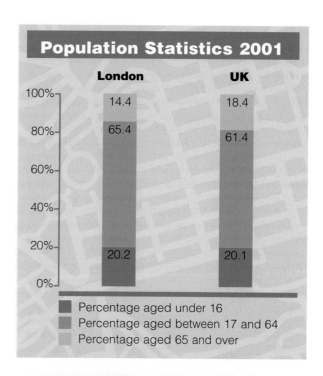

Population Statistics 2001

	London	UK
Percentage aged 65 and over	14.4	18.4
Percentage aged between 17 and 64	65.4	61.4
Percentage aged under 16	20.2	20.1

■ Percentage aged under 16
■ Percentage aged between 17 and 64
■ Percentage aged 65 and over

▶ *A fish stall in Brixton market in south London, where the local population is mostly Afro-Caribbean. The stalls sell Caribbean fruits and vegetables, as well as CDs, clothes, and household goods.*

Diverse Communities

Part of the rich diversity of London comes from the fact that Britain once ruled the largest colonial empire in the world. Thousands of people from former British colonies in the Caribbean, Africa, and South Asia have come to settle in London. They and their descendants form their own distinct communities, but over the years they have also become established as Londoners.

The Afro-Caribbean Community

Afro-Caribbean people can trace their origins to Africa, from which their ancestors traveled (most often as slaves) to the islands of the Caribbean Sea. These islands, mainly Jamaica, Trinidad, and Barbados, have been British territories since as long ago as the 1600s. Many Afro-Caribbeans came to London in the 1950s, responding to recruitment drives for the new National Health Service and for London Transport. Other Londoners did not always welcome the newcomers, and it was often difficult for them to find decent jobs or homes. Now, Afro-Caribbean families live in all parts of London, with strong communities in Brixton and Peckham in south London, and Harlesden and Willesden in north London.

The South Asian Community

London's South Asians came originally from India, Pakistan, Bangladesh, and Sri Lanka. Most arrived in the 1960s and 1970s in search of work and security. Often the men

▲ *Shopping in Whitechapel, in the East End. Many of the first wave of Bangladeshis who came to Britain in the 1960s and 1970s settled in Whitechapel.*

arrived first, with their wives and families following later. They have settled in many parts of London, with established Indian communities in Southall and Ealing in west London, and Bangladeshi and Pakistani communities in the East End. The borough of Tower Hamlets in east London is home to more than fifty thousand Bangladeshis, the largest number in Europe.

The South Asian communities have introduced different religious traditions into London, and today many places of worship cater to their different needs, including Hindu temples, Sikh gurdwaras, and Islamic mosques. Regent's Park is home to the beautiful London Central Mosque.

The Shri Swaminarayan Temple

The Shri Swaminarayan Mandir in Neasden, northwest London (below), is the largest traditional Hindu temple outside India, and is sometimes called one of the wonders of the modern world. It was built in 1995 at a cost of about £10 million (U.S. $15 million). The temple's ornate carvings of Hindu gods and goddesses were created in India by more than 1,500 skilled craftspeople.

Chinatown

Many of London's Chinese residents first arrived in the 1950s and 1960s. A run-down part of Soho, where property prices were cheap, soon became the heart of their community. Today, only a few Chinese people live in London's Chinatown, but it provides the focus for cultural and social gatherings for Chinese families, especially on Sundays. It is a unique, bustling part of London's West End.

Festivals and Celebrations

London has many music, dance, and film festivals throughout the year. London's different communities often have their own special religious and cultural celebrations. Today, some of these have become popular events, shared by Londoners from all walks of life.

The annual celebration of Chinese New Year takes place in January or February. Once a small community event on Chinatown's Gerrard Street, it now spills out into Leicester Square and Trafalgar Square. Huge paper dragons snake their way along the crowded streets, decorated with brightly colored lanterns and flags. As the event has grown, Chinese music and opera, and demonstrations of martial arts, have been added.

The Notting Hill Carnival, the largest street festival in Europe, takes place during the last weekend in August. It began in the 1960s as a small community celebration of Caribbean culture. Today, during the festival, the streets of Notting Hill are packed with more than one million revelers from all backgrounds and cultures.

The main events are the dazzling parades of masqueraders, with a special children's parade on Sunday. The dancing masqueraders are accompanied by steel

◄ *A masquerader at the Notting Hill Carnival. Many people spend months working on their elaborate costumes.*

bands, calypso songs, and soca music, a cross between soul and calypso.

Bonfire Night

Bonfire Night is the closest thing to an Independence Day celebration in Britain. The festival marks the failure of the 1605 Gunpowder Plot to destroy Parliament, led by Guy Fawkes. Every November 5, Londoners light bonfires and set off fireworks. Some still follow the ancient tradition of burning a symbolic dummy—the "Guy"—on top of the bonfire.

Christmas and New Year

The days before Christmas are a special time in London, especially for children. The Christmas lights of Regent Street and Oxford Street brighten up the long winter evenings. Store windows are beautifully decorated, especially those of famous stores

▲ *Christmas lights on Regent Street. Every year a different celebrity is invited to switch on the lights in a special ceremony.*

such as Selfridge's, Liberty, and Hamleys, the world's largest toy store.

Concerts and festivals of carols are held in candlelit churches, including St. Paul's Cathedral and Westminster Abbey, as well as Christmas plays and pantomimes. In Trafalgar Square, carol singers gather under the huge Christmas tree given every year by the people of Norway to thank the British for their support during World War II.

Trafalgar Square is also at the heart of London's New Year celebrations. On New Year's Eve, large crowds of people gather to hear the chimes of Westminster's famous bell, Big Ben, ring in the new year and to sing the traditional refrain of "Auld Lang Syne."

CHAPTER 3

Living in London

Londoners live in many different types of homes. Some live in apartments in high-rise buildings. Sometimes large, older houses are converted into two or more separate apartments, or "flats." There are also row houses, semidetached houses (two houses attached by an adjoining wall), and detached houses (houses with no other buildings adjoining them).

Most houses in London today were built after 1700, as the population of London grew rapidly. About one-quarter of London's housing was built in the nineteenth century. In the twentieth century, more public housing, known as "council" housing, was built. Council houses were small, basic in style, and rented to low-income families.

Tower Blocks

The shortage of housing in London after World War II encouraged architects and planners to build apartments in tall high-rise buildings known as "tower blocks." They offered poorer families the opportunity to move away from old slums dating back to the Victorian era. But many tower blocks fell into disrepair, and became bleak and unattractive places to live. In recent years, some tower blocks have been demolished, while others have been remodeled mainly for young, single people or couples.

◀ *One side of London life—the Harrow Road part of west London. Here low-rise apartment buildings crowd together, with few green spaces between.*

Rich and Poor

London has rich and poor areas. Many wealthy people live in or near the West End, with its fine, large houses, quiet squares, and gardens. In the East End, the housing is often in poor repair. However, some previously run-down areas have become fashionable in recent years, especially where there has been new office or business development. Along the Thames River in the Docklands area, old warehouses have been redesigned as luxury flats, with views over the river. Lofts with open-plan living space have become "trendy."

Housing Problems

Unlike many other capital city dwellers, Londoners usually try to buy their own homes rather than rent. However, London property prices are the highest in Britain, sometimes twice as much as in other cities or regions. Many people who do not earn large salaries can no longer afford to live in London. Commuting into London is costly and transportation systems often suffer delays. As a result, there is a growing shortage of workers in essential services, such as nurses, teachers, firefighters, and police officers, who are moving out of London and choosing to work in less expensive communities.

▶ *The other side of London life. These brightly colored row houses are in Chelsea, one of London's most expensive and exclusive areas.*

The Big Issue

To aid those without homes, several London charities provide food and advice and help homeless people find temporary accommodation in shelters. Many homeless people earn money by selling the Big Issue, a magazine produced solely for homeless people to sell. The Big Issue features a mix of news, reviews, poetry, and commentary, and part of the price of each copy goes to the seller. The magazine offers a step back up on the ladder to work and finding a home.

Shopping and Food

London has literally thousands of places to shop. Central London has famous shopping areas, such as Oxford Street and Regent Street. More exclusive and expensive shops are found in Knightsbridge, including Harrods, Europe's largest department store. There are also streets that specialize in certain goods, such as secondhand books on Charing Cross Road and electronics on Tottenham Court Road.

Covent Garden was once London's biggest market for fruit and vegetables. Today, it houses small shops, stalls, and a covered market called the Jubilee Market. With its street entertainers, cafes, and restaurants, it has become one of London's most popular tourist areas.

Fortnum and Mason is a unique department store on Piccadilly, a street in the West End. Started in 1707 by William Fortnum, a footman in the royal household, and his landlord, Hugh Mason, the store has specialized in selling luxury goods for nearly three hundred years. It catered in its early years to the royal family and wealthy West-Enders. Fortnum and Mason is best known for its range of fine foods and luxury hampers, large wicker baskets filled with champagne and delicacies, often exchanged by wealthy Londoners as Christmas gifts.

Street Markets

London has more than sixty street markets. Petticoat Lane in the East End is one of London's most famous traditional markets, offering over a thousand stalls each Sunday. Columbia Road Market, also a Sunday market, is in the East End and sells only flowers and plants. In Notting Hill, the mile-long (1.6 km-long) Portobello Market is especially popular for its antiques stalls.

Dining Out

Londoners love eating out and often go to restaurants serving food from all parts of the globe. Although many European-style cafes and bars have opened in recent years, the English tradition of taking afternoon tea continues, mostly in large hotels and

◄ *Tourists browse at a stall in the Jubilee Market in Covent Garden.*

Pubs

The "public house," or "pub"—a traditional British bar—has been an essential part of London life for hundreds of years. Old historic pubs still exist, such as the George Inn in Southwark, one of London's original coaching inns for travelers. The Dickens Inn, built in an eighteenth-century warehouse, is located near Tower Bridge, and the Mayflower Inn at Rotherhithe is near where the Mayflower first set sail. Most London pubs now offer food as well as beverages; some have also become venues for live music, comedy clubs, and fringe theater.

department stores. Afternoon tea can be quite a lavish affair, involving various types of tea in china cups, smoked salmon sandwiches, cakes, and "crumpets," a type of toasted muffin.

Take-out dinners have become part of British life. Many fast food places offer burgers, pizzas, kebabs, Indian curries, and Chinese meals. One of Britain's traditional fast foods, fish and chips, is still a favorite takeout.

▼ *Oxford Street is the site of many of London's best department stores, including Marks and Spencer, and Selfridge's (on the right).*

Education in London

Children under the age of sixteen account for over 20 percent of the population of London. Young children may go to playgroups or kindergarten from the age of two. Children then start elementary, or "primary," school at four or five and move on to secondary school (junior high and high school) at eleven. Most London children go to comprehensive schools, which are schools paid for by local councils. Education is compulsory until sixteen.

The school day usually begins about 9:00 A.M. and finishes between 3:00 and 4:00 in the afternoon. All London students follow the National Curriculum for England and Wales, which sets out what subjects they should study and how they should study them. Students have to take regular tests to check that they have achieved the agreed-upon standards in the curriculum.

Schools in London face particular challenges. Many have pupils from a range of backgrounds who speak different languages and follow different religious faiths. The high cost of living in the capital and discipline problems in schools have led to a growing shortage of teachers in London.

Some London children go to private schools known as "independent" schools or—confusingly—as "public" schools. These charge a fee, and many are for either boys or girls. For parents who can afford it, they offer a high standard of education. Some of the United Kingdom's most famous

▲ These boys, in their distinctive uniform and "boaters" (hats) are from Harrow School in north London, one of the country's most famous "public" schools.

independent schools are in London. These include Harrow in north London and Westminster in the heart of the city.

The British education system is quite different from the U.S. system. At sixteen, British children reduce the number of subjects they are taught to two or three—called "A" levels—and study only those subjects until age eighteen. This system was introduced to prepare students for further specialization at the university level.

After School

London offers many exciting after-school activities for children. Some theaters arrange children's workshops or put on puppet shows and Christmas pantomimes. Outdoor excursions can include city farms, children's zoos, and parks. Museums specially designed for children, such as Pollock's Toy Museum near Tottenham Court Road, also are popular.

Higher Education

The University of London is the largest university in the United Kingdom, with about one hundred thousand students. London has a strong reputation for medical education, with several teaching hospitals. University College, founded in 1826, is the oldest college in London and was the first in the country to accept women.

London also has many colleges that specialize in subjects in the creative arts,

▲ *Children on the playground of Islington Junior School, in north London.*

such as art, fashion, and design, as well as drama, music, and dance. The Royal Ballet School trains some of the most talented young classical ballet dancers in the world. Students follow an eight-year dance course and they often start classes at the school at the age of eleven.

The Royal Academy of Music, founded in 1822, prepares students for a professional career in music. Its graduates go on to become solo and orchestral musicians, opera singers, conductors, and composers. Famous alumni include popular singer and songwriter Elton John, conductor Sir Simon Rattle, and composer Sir John Barbirolli.

London also offers great opportunities for lifelong learning. Evening classes are available throughout the capital in almost any subject imaginable.

CHAPTER 4

London at Work

London has a long history as one of the great trading centers of the world. Much of Britain's global import and export trade once came through the docks to the east of London Bridge. By the mid-twentieth century, London's manufacturing industries and docks had begun to decline. Today it is estimated that about eight out of every ten working Londoners is employed in service industries such as catering, tourism, the media, local and national government, communications, and transportation. Among the most important are the financial and

Tourism

Tourism is a vital part of London's economy. The tourist industry employs about 8 percent of London's workforce, including people who work as tourist guides, in hotels, in gift shops, and at major tourist attractions. The number of tourists in the year 2000 totaled 31.6 million. Of these, 18.5 million were from other parts of Britain and 13.1 million were from overseas. Tourists who stayed in London spent nearly $15 billion in 2000. London is a very popular destination for American tourists. In 2000 nearly 3 million Americans visited London, over 20 percent of all overseas visitors. Next came France (just under 10 percent), and Germany (about 8.5 percent).

◄ *The internationally renowned insurance institution Lloyd's of London is based in an award-winning office building, designed and built in the 1980s.*

business sectors, both in terms of the numbers of people employed and the amount of wealth created.

Business and Finance in London

London, particularly the Square Mile of the City, is the financial heart of the United Kingdom. It is, alongside New York and Tokyo, one of three main global financial centers. For hundreds of years, national and international business was carried out in its narrow streets, taverns, and coffee houses. Today, modern office buildings have replaced many of the old ones, including the shimmering steel pipes and glass of the Lloyd's of London building. Every day thousands of people pour into the City of London to work, deserting it at night. Only seven thousand people actually live there.

London has more international banks than any other financial center. The biggest and most important of these is the Bank of England. Set up over three hundred years ago, it is the central bank of the United Kingdom. It issues currency notes, sets interest rates, and stores all of Britain's huge gold reserves in its high-security vaults.

The Stock Exchange is where company shares are bought and sold. Trading formerly took place on the floor of the Exchange, with the city traders shouting out the prices of the different shares. Today much of the verbal trading has been replaced by computer and telephone deals from separate dealing rooms.

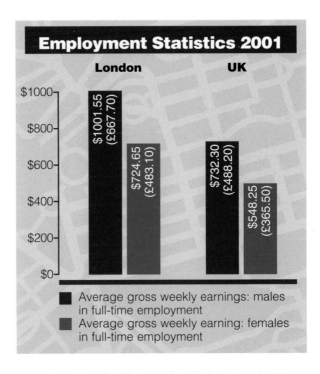

Employment Statistics 2001

London   UK

$1001.55 (£667.70)
$724.65 (£483.10)
$732.30 (£488.20)
$548.25 (£365.50)

■ Average gross weekly earnings: males in full-time employment
■ Average gross weekly earning: females in full-time employment

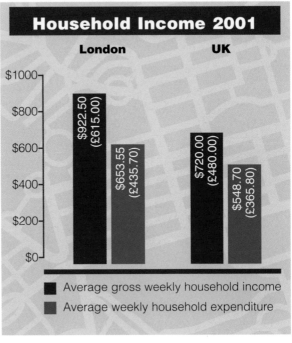

Household Income 2001

London   UK

$922.50 (£615.00)
$653.55 (£435.70)
$720.00 (£480.00)
$548.70 (£365.80)

■ Average gross weekly household income
■ Average weekly household expenditure

▲ *Londoners earn significantly more than people living in other parts of the country.*

A Media-Savvy City

The different aspects of the media—newspapers, television, and radio—flourish in London and provide employment for many thousands of the city's workers.

Most of the United Kingdom's national newspapers are published in London. For centuries, the heart of the newspaper publishing industry was on Fleet Street. In the 1980s, however, almost all the newspapers moved their offices to the refurbished Docklands.

Serious "broadsheet" (large-format) national newspapers such as the *Times*, the *Independent*, and the *Guardian*, offer news and comment from home and overseas. Smaller-sized "tabloids," such as the *Sun* and the *Daily Mail*, have less news and carry a lot more celebrity gossip, scandal, and sports. The *Evening Standard* is a daily paper that focuses on London. For people who want even more locally relevant information, each of the London boroughs produces papers with the area news, details of local events, and ads.

For essential information on music, film, and theater, Londoners turn to the weekly events magazine *Time Out*. There are also specialized newspapers for different ethnic communities, such as the *Irish Post*; the *Voice* of the Afro-Caribbean community; and the *Jewish Chronicle*, first published in 1841 and the oldest Jewish newspaper in the world.

▼ *Londoners from different ethnic backgrounds have newspapers that address their specific concerns in their own language, like this one in Bengali.*

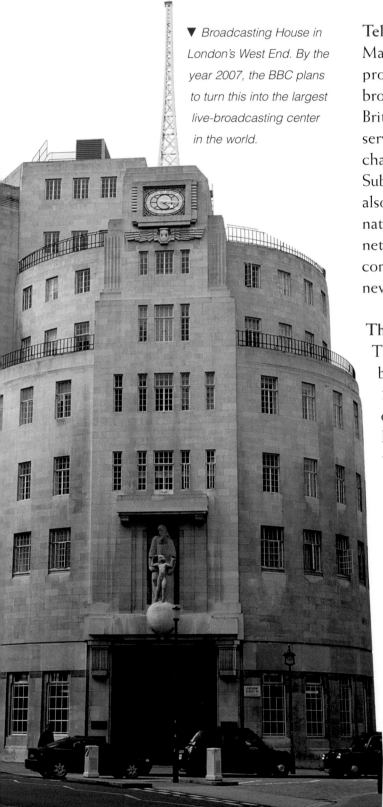

▼ Broadcasting House in London's West End. By the year 2007, the BBC plans to turn this into the largest live-broadcasting center in the world.

Television and Radio

Many British television programs are produced in London. Britain has five broadcast channels, including two BBC—British Broadcasting Corporation—public service channels and three independent channels that are funded by advertising. Subscription satellite and cable channels are also gaining popularity. Many local and national radio stations are part of the BBC's network; others are advertisement-funded commercial stations offering music, local news, and "phone-ins," or talk shows.

The British Broadcasting Corporation

The British Broadcasting Corporation first began transmitting radio programs in 1922. The BBC Television Centre operates from west London, while Broadcasting House and Bush House, which focus mostly on radio, are in London's West End. In spite of many changes over the years, the BBC has maintained its reputation as possibly the world's most respected public service broadcaster of both radio and television. Today, the BBC faces enormous competition from other channels, including broadcast, cable, and satellite. It has recently expanded into the new area of digital broadcasting. Most of the funding for the BBC comes from annual license fees paid by every British person who owns a television. The BBC carries no advertising.

Transportation in London

Traveling around London is a challenge, whatever system of transportation a person chooses to use. Buses, taxis, cars, and trucks all crowd onto London's roads. Some commuters drive to work, but finding somewhere to park is difficult and expensive. More one-way streets and parking restrictions have been introduced in an effort to reduce traffic. In addition, new, wider roads have been built, including a six-lane freeway around London, the M25 motorway. In spite of these measures, the amount of traffic has increased and the problem remains. In February 2003 the Greater London Assembly introduced a toll, called the congestion charge, for all motorists driving into central London during busy times, hoping to reduce the number of cars and raise money for public transportation.

The "Tube"

London's subway system, often called the Underground, or the "tube," has twelve different lines and nearly three hundred stations crisscrossing London and stretching out into the suburbs. At least half of the underground system is actually above ground. The majority of Londoners travel to work by tube, and the trains can become very crowded and hot during the morning and evening rush hours.

On the Buses

There are hundreds of different bus routes across London. Most of London's buses are still the famous red double-deckers. Open-top tourist buses go past the main London attractions. Several all-night bus services start from Trafalgar Square.

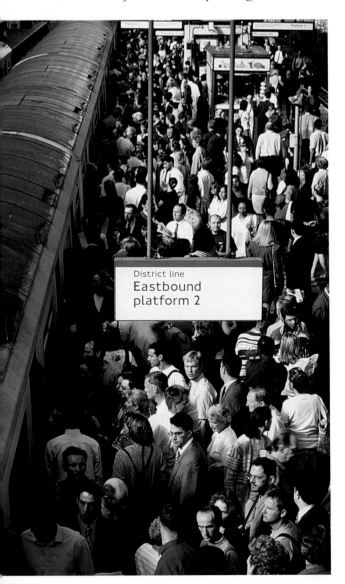

◄ Commuters jostle for space at Earl's Court station, on the London Underground's District Line.

Rail Travel

London has twelve main railway stations, which all connect to the Underground. London's first railway line was opened in the 1830s to bring commuters into their central London workplaces. The Docklands Light Railway (DLR), opened by the queen in 1987, connects the City with the Docklands and east London. The DLR uses driverless trains controlled by computer. And, using the Eurostar high-speed rail link under the English Channel, Londoners can reach Paris, France, within three hours.

Air Travel

London has four airports. The largest is Heathrow, some 15 mi (24 km) west of London. It is the busiest airport in the world, with over 60 million passengers in 2000–2001 and an average of 1,200 flights a day. Other London airports are Gatwick, Stansted, and City Airport.

◀ *Buses caught in traffic gridlock on a London street. Special bus lanes now speed up travel times.*

About eighteen thousand licensed taxis operate in London, most of them black. Fares are not cheap, but London "cabbies" are the best trained in Europe. Before receiving their licenses, they spend up to two years learning what is called the "knowledge" on all the routes around London.

Governing London

Local government for London is divided between the local boroughs, the Corporation of the City of London, and the Greater London Authority (this includes the London Assembly and the mayor).

Local Boroughs

All the boroughs of London have their own councils, which are responsible for local services, such as education, social services, housing, and roads, as well as facilities for sports and culture. Their spending budgets come partly from the national government and partly from local taxes. Local elections are held every four years. Residents of the different boroughs can vote for councillors put forward by local and national political parties. Councils are often made up of members of several different parties, and the party with the majority of councillors often dictates local policies.

The Corporation of the City of London

The City has its own laws and system of local government, which are independent from the rest of London. The Corporation of the City of London is the oldest local authority in Britain, and it continues to follow its ancient traditions. Members of the Corporation's governing bodies—the Court of Common Council and the Court of Aldermen—are elected by City residents and businesses. In addition to the usual services provided by a council, such as

housing, trash collection, education, and social services, the two councils run the City's police force and the nation's Central Criminal Court. They also maintain five Thames bridges and run the quarantine station at Heathrow Airport.

The Court of Common Council, which is the Corporation's primary decision-making assembly, meets every four weeks. Common Council members are elected every year in December by divisions of the City called wards. Each ward elects between four and twelve members, depending on its size.

There are also twenty-five members of the Court of Aldermen. Each alderman is elected by one City ward. They do not belong to any political party, and once chosen, they stay in office for life. They serve on Common Council committees and also act as governors and trustees of schools, hospitals, and charities. Every year, they elect a new Lord Mayor.

The Lord Mayor presides over the Court of Aldermen and the Court of Common Council. He or she is Chief Magistrate of the City of London, Admiral of the Port of London, Chancellor of City University, and patron of many civic and charitable organizations. It is also his or her responsibility to promote the City's business role on a national and international level.

The Mayor and the London Assembly

The Square Mile of the City has long had its own Lord Mayor, but it was only in the year

2000 that a mayor in the usual sense was elected for Greater London. The mayor and the twenty-five-member London Assembly make up the Greater London Authority. The mayor has broad responsibilities for all of London, including transportation, the police, economic development, planning, culture, and the environment. With a budget of $5.5 billion, the mayor sets annual budgets for the London Fire and Emergency Planning Authority, the new Transport for London (which now runs the city's transportation services, except the Underground), the Metropolitan Police, and the London Development Agency, which promotes London-based businesses. The mayor also controls two of London's most important public spaces—Trafalgar Square and Parliament Square.

The London Assembly, based at City Hall, works with the mayor, making recommendations on issues important to Londoners. It also examines the mayor's decisions. All meetings are held in public. Londoners can vote for a new mayor and Assembly every four years. Ken Livingstone, the first London mayor, was elected in 2000.

▼ *City Hall, the new home of the mayor and London Assembly, opened in 2002. Its energy-efficient design makes it one of the "greenest" buildings in London.*

CHAPTER 5

London at Play

It could take a lifetime to get to know all of London's world-class museums, fine art galleries, and other attractions.

Theater

In the West End, the larger theaters put on classical and modern plays, musicals, and thrillers. The National Theatre on the South Bank has three theaters of different sizes. Theatergoers can also enjoy more unusual, experimental plays in the smaller off-West End and fringe theaters.

Music

There is live music every night of the week in London. The number of music festivals and open-air concerts has increased greatly in recent years, with performances in churches, parks, and pubs. For classical music and opera, top venues include the Royal Festival Hall, the Royal Opera House, and the Albert Hall, which every summer hosts the hugely popular BBC "Proms." This is a series of afternoon and evening concerts featuring a mixture of classical and contemporary music. The Last Night of the Proms is one of the main cultural events of London's summer concert season. While the performers play patriotic music, the audience—waving streamers, balloons, British flags, and conductors' batons—joins in with whistles, trumpets, and loud, often raucous, singing.

◀ *Inside Tower Bridge, visitors can view the original Victorian engine rooms.*

Museums

During Britain's colonial past, treasures from around the world were brought to London as trophies. For this reason, London has today a wealth of internationally renowned museums, which are sometimes found in clusters in central London. On Exhibition Road in Kensington, people can visit the Victoria and Albert Museum, the Science Museum, and the Natural History Museum.

The British Museum is one of the greatest museums in the world, containing some four million objects, from Egyptian mummies to artifacts from classical Greece and Rome. Among its most famous exhibits are the Elgin Marbles—the great stone sculptures from the Parthenon temple in Greece—and the Rosetta Stone, with its Egyptian hieroglyphs.

The world-famous Madame Tussaud's Wax Museum is one of London's most popular tourist attractions. Visitors stand in line, sometimes for hours, to see the lifelike wax figures of famous people, from modern pop stars to historical figures.

Bankside: Old and New

Several new and refurbished buildings have revitalized the area along the Thames River, known as Bankside.

The Tate Modern, converted from an old power station, opened in 2000. It is now the most popular museum of modern art in the world, with over five million visitors in its first year alone.

▲ *The Natural History Museum holds over 70 million specimens, most unseen by the general public.*

Alongside the Tate Modern is the Globe, a life-size replica of the original theater where many of William Shakespeare's plays were first performed over four hundred years ago. Many members of the audience stand, just as they did in Shakespeare's day. Plays are staged here only during the summer.

The Millennium Bridge is the first pedestrian-only bridge to cross the Thames River. It links two of the oldest parts of London: Bankside and the City.

"The [Millennium] Bridge will be lit at night to form a blade of light across the Thames."

—Sir Norman Foster, chief architect of the Millennium Bridge.

London Outdoors

For a city of its size, London has a remarkable number and variety of green spaces, including the Royal Parks, local parks, woods, city farms, and private gardens. London's many allotments allow people to enjoy growing their own vegetables, herbs, or flowers on a small plot of land rented to them at a very cheap rate by their local council.

Parks

Hyde Park, which is London's largest park; Green Park; and St. James's Park all link together to form a "green belt" running through the heart of London. Further north is Regent's Park, home of the London Zoo and an open-air theater.

"The Thames is still at the heart of London life. It is cleaner than it has been for 150 years and is the least polluted estuary of any metropolitan river in the world.... We regard the quality of the capital's urban environment as central to its economic success. It is therefore vital that we maintain and develop this precious asset."

—Michael Ward, chief executive of the London Development Agency, June 2002.

▼ *A test match at Lord's Cricket Ground. Test matches can last up to six days.*

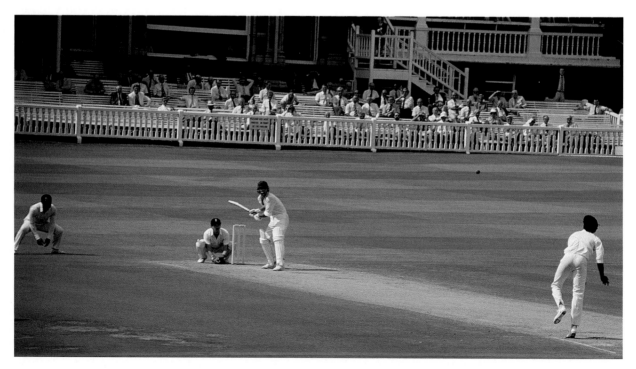

▲ *The greenhouses of Kew Gardens are as impressive as the plants that grow in them.*

Located outside the center of London, Richmond Park is Europe's largest city park, with almost 2,500 acres (1,000 hectares) of grassland and woods. It is famed for its herds of deer and for its ancient oak trees.

Kew Gardens, home of the Royal Botanical Society, has the most diverse plant collection in the world, with more than 40,000 different varieties of plants and trees.

Sports

Soccer—or "football" as it is known in Britain—is a great passion for many Londoners. The capital usually has between four and six clubs in Britain's Premier League.

For tennis fans, the highlight of the year is Wimbledon, one of the world's top tennis tournaments. Wimbledon is a great British tradition, with its grass courts, unpredictable summer weather, and strawberries and cream.

Other summer events include test match cricket (games/series played against teams from other countries) at Lord's and the Oval—two traditional cricket stadiums—and international track-and-field events at Crystal Palace. Winter events include rugby at Twickenham and the Oxford and Cambridge Boat Race. Every March, for over 150 years, rowers from the rival universities of Oxford and Cambridge have competed along a 4-mi (6-km) stretch of the Thames River.

The London Marathon is the biggest marathon event in the world. Every April, about 30,000 runners line up to run 26 mi (42 km) from Greenwich to Westminster. Many competitors run for charity, and some wear humorous costumes.

Londoners also have access to a huge range of sporting facilities, from public exercise centers to expensive private gyms. Many of London's parks have playing fields for soccer, cricket, and baseball, as well as tennis courts.

CHAPTER 6

Looking Forward

London's population has been growing rapidly in recent years. Between 1981 and 2001, the population grew by 5.4 percent, from 6,805,600 to 7,172,036. Population experts calculate that by 2016, it will grow by another 700,000. More young people are coming to live in London. The number of refugees and asylum seekers arriving in London is also increasing. If housing costs continue to rise, more lower- and middle-income families will be forced to leave the city.

Homes and Housing

With a growing population and more single-person households, London will need more than an estimated twenty-three thousand additional homes each year until 2016 to meet its housing requirements. The pressing need for more affordable housing has spurred plans to develop new types of homes. Micro-housing is one example: small, space-saving units designed for single people or couples. There are also plans to build on unused "brownfield" sites where land has previously been used for industry.

The London Eye

This giant ferris wheel (left) opened in January 2000, in celebration of the new millennium. At nearly 450 ft (140 m) high and with thirty-two enclosed capsules, it is the largest observational wheel in the world. As it slowly rotates, the wheel offers a spectacular bird's-eye view of the landmarks of London.

Transportation

London's transportation system is run down and under pressure, leading to ambitious, sometimes controversial, plans to improve public transportation and reduce road traffic. London's local councils have often disagreed about the amount of investment needed and whether funding should come from the government or private investors.

Nevertheless, many improvements are already under way, such as a great increase in bus services. The new high-speed Channel Tunnel Rail Link from St. Pancras Station is due to open in 2007. The journey time from London to Paris then will be only two hours and twenty minutes. A major Crossrail service, providing fast, direct rail journeys from east to west London, is being planned. London's network of cycle routes and river travel also are being improved to encourage more "green" travel.

However, current plans to modernize the Underground have met with hostility from workers' unions and the mayor. This is because of government attempts to privatize the system (allow private companies to run certain parts of the Underground) in exchange for funds to renovate.

Redevelopment

Run-down areas of London are being redeveloped to provide new homes, jobs, business opportunities, leisure facilities, and better transportation. In west London, the Paddington Basin development will restore

▲ *The high-speed Eurostar service is a model for the development of London's transportation system.*

the canal and surrounding land polluted by industry. In east London, the Greenwich Millennium Village will rejuvenate the area around the Millennium Dome. Branded an "eco-friendly" development, the village will feature fourteen hundred new homes, modern transportation links into the city center, 50 acres (20.24 ha) of parkland, an ecology park, a multiplex cinema, and shops. And, in central London, it is hoped the increase in passenger traffic from the new Channel Tunnel Rail Link will regenerate the King's Cross area.

At the beginning of the third millennium, London, like all modern cities, faces many challenges. Yet the city and its people will continue to adapt, as they have throughout the capital's two-thousand-year history.

Time Line

A.D. 43 The Romans arrive in Britain and establish Londinium.

60–61 Boudicca attacks Roman towns and Londinium is destroyed.

886 The Anglo-Saxon King Alfred the Great captures London from the Danes.

1065 Edward the Confessor completes the building of an abbey and palace at Westminster.

1066 The Normans invade England and capture London; William the Conqueror is crowned at Westminster Abbey.

1215 The first Lord Mayor of the City of London is elected.

1348–1349 The Black Death kills more than half of London's population.

1605 The Gunpowder Plot to blow up the Houses of Parliament fails.

1665 The Great Plague kills nearly 80,000 Londoners.

1666 The Great Fire destroys four-fifths of London.

1667–1709 London is rebuilt; Christopher Wren designs St. Paul's Cathedral.

1732 10 Downing Street becomes the official residence of Britain's prime minister.

1822 The Royal Academy of Music is founded in London.

1826 University College, the first university in Britain to accept women, is founded in London.

1845–48 Many Irish immigrants move to London following the Great Potato Famine.

1940–1941 During the German "Blitz" of London, nearly 10,000 Londoners die.

1945–1960 London is rebuilt after the war; Britain gives up its vast empire; Queen Elizabeth II comes to the throne in 1952; immigrants from the British Commonwealth arrive in London.

1960s "Swinging" London becomes an international focus of popular culture.

2000 Ken Livingstone is elected first mayor of London. The London Eye and the Millennium Bridge open.

2002 City Hall becomes the new seat of the Greater London Authority.

2003 The congestion charge is activated to reduce traffic in central London.

Glossary

amphitheater an open structure with a circular or oval arena. In Roman times, contests were held in amphitheaters.

Anglo-Saxons Germanic-speaking people who settled in England after the decline of Roman rule. "Anglo-Saxon" was later used to refer to English people.

asylum seekers people fleeing their own country, often for political reasons, in search of a safe place to live and work.

bearbaiting a form of entertainment in which dogs were encouraged to attack a chained bear. Bearbaiting was outlawed in Britain in the nineteenth century.

borough a division of a town or city, such as London, with its own local government.

British Isles the islands of Great Britain, Ireland, the Hebrides, the Orkneys, Shetland, the Isle of Man, the Isle of Wight, the Scilly Isles, and the Channel Islands.

Celts of Indo-European descent. The main inhabitants of the British Isles before the Roman invasion.

cholera a highly infectious disease spread through unclean water or food; affects the intestines and causes death if left untreated.

cockfight a sport where cockerels (young roosters) were made to fight each other.

colony a territory settled by people from another land.

commuter a person who travels to work.

coronation the crowning of a monarch.

county the subdivision of a territory into separately governed units.

cricket a game similar to baseball.

Cypriot a person from the island of Cyprus in the Mediterranean.

epidemic an outbreak of an infectious disease that spreads quickly and affects many people in a community or larger region.

exports goods sold to other countries.

fringe theater theatrical productions that are more adventurous than most plays, performed in small theaters and other venues.

hieroglyphs a form of writing, found mostly in ancient Egypt, that uses symbols or pictures to represent words.

imports goods bought from other countries.

Industrial Revolution an era when the invention of new machines meant that goods could be produced in factories at a faster rate and in much larger quantities than in craft workshops.

interest rates the rate at which interest, a fee charged when people borrow money or use credit, is calculated. The interest rate is usually a percentage of the amount of money borrowed.

magistrate a citizen with good public standing who is given a position of judicial authority over others.

Millennium Dome an exhibition center constructed for the 2000 millennium celebrations in London.

monarch a ruler of a country, such as a king or queen, who has a right to the title by birth and is not elected.

monastery a building in which monks live.

pantomimes a type of play for children with music, funny songs, and outrageous costumes, which is usually performed during Christmastime.

Parliament the highest lawmaking authority in Britain, made up of the House of Commons, the House of Lords, and the ruling king or queen. Members of the House of Commons are elected by the people, and serve as the main lawmaking body.

Parthenon a famous temple in Athens, Greece, dedicated to the Greek goddess Athena; built nearly 2,500 years ago.

prime minister the highest elected representative of the British government.

quarantine a place where people or animals suspected of having a disease are separated from the general population, to stop the spread of the illness to others.

rugby a game similar to American football, but players wear no protective padding.

slum a run-down, dirty area, usually in a city, where poor people live in crowded, substandard housing.

smallpox an infectious disease spread by air or contact, causing a high fever and spots on the skin. Before vaccinations, about four of every ten people with smallpox died.

smog smoke or pollution mixed with fog.

stocks and shares stocks, representing the worth of a company's money and equipment, are broken down into shares, which can be bought and sold. Shareholders then own rights to that company.

thriller drama or fiction that builds interest by using suspense, intrigue, or adventure.

traders people who buy and sell goods; in the City of London, people who buy and sell shares in different companies.

typhus an infectious disease spread by fleas and lice in unclean conditions and which causes high fever, headaches, and a rash.

vaudeville stage entertainment featuring a variety of acts, including singing, dancing, acrobatics, and comedy.

ward a division of a city for administrative or electoral purposes.

Further Information

Books

Adams, Simon. *Kid's London*. Dorling Kindersley Travel Guides, 2000.

Butterfield, Moira. *Usborne Book of London*. EDC Publications, 1987.

Fallon, Steve. *London Condensed (Lonely Planet Condensed Guides)*. Lonely Planet, 2002.

Leapman, Michael. *Eyewitness Travel Guide: London*. Dorling Kindersley, 2003.

Sobel Spirn, Michele. *The Bridges in London (Going to)*. Four Corners Publishing, 2000.

Time Out London Guide. Penguin, 2002.

Toht, David W. and Betony, and Webb, Ray. *Daily Life in Ancient and Modern London (Cities through Time)*. Runestone Press, 2001.

Web Sites

http://www.netlondon.com
London's Internet directory, for general information.

http://britannia.com/travel/london/index.html
An American Internet guide to the British Isles.

http://www.museum-london.org.uk/
The Museum of London's web site, which offers helpful links to other museums and places to visit.

http://www.nhm.ac.uk
The Natural History Museum's exhibit information.

http://www.british-museum.ac.uk
The British Museum's site, with exhibit pictures.

http://www.shakespeares-globe.org
Theater organization site with a pictorial tour of the reconstructed Globe Theatre and complete history.

Index

Page numbers in **bold** indicate pictures.